A COLLECTION OF POEMS

ANAPHORA
AND EPIPHORA

Published By

Poets Choice
www.poetschoice.in

First Edition January 2023

Poems in this book are from:

United States   Canada   Nigeria   Ukraine   India   Fiji

Special Thanks:
Therese Kosterman • Jordan VanDerlinde • Donna Harlan •
Katherine Musgrave • Michael Angelone • Lisa Ochoa

No Winnes

Cover Designed By Koni Deraz, Germany
Back Cover Content By Akshay Sonthalia, India
Book Designed By Laura Antonioli, England
Edited By Dante Antonio, United States
Selection Editor Tarun Agarwal, India

ISBN: 978-93-95193-46-7

BCID: 991-16768705

Visit www.bookcrossing.com

Price
$32 USD

POEMS

A Body Can

Jordan VanDerLinde
Glendale, California - United States

Breathe in, breathe out
    walk to the end of the driveway, grab the paper,
    cook breakfast, fill early morning with eggs & oregano.
Breathe in, breathe out
    decide it's time to go, take too long to leave,
    mosey down the jetbridge at the sound of last boarding call.
Breathe in, breathe out
    run to get the phone before it quits ringing,
    give directions to a misplaced tourist on Fifth Avenue.
Breathe in, breathe out
    dip a child's toes in the ocean for the first time,
    throw up off the side of a deepsea fishing boat
Breathe in, breathe out
    survive cancer,
    amputation,
    sepsis.
Breathe in, breathe out
    imagine a future.

Breathe in, breathe out
    call someone, a favorite person to talk to,
Breathe in, breathe out
    wrap its arms around another body,
Breathe in, breathe out
    until its finished.
    Until it can't anymore.

A Nurse

Crystal Barker

North Las Vegas, Nevada - United States

She became a nurse,
    innocent, idealistic,
    her passion aflame.

She became a nurse
    to help the sick and lame.

She became a nurse,
    then COVID came.
    Some left the bedside,
    but she'd remain.
    She did not complain.
    Health and energy began to wane;
    eventually overcome
    from the strain.

She became a nurse
    To help the sick and lame—
    sacrificed her life for those she served,
    without glory or fame;
    and left this world early,
    in a six-by-three wooden-frame.

Agoraphobia

Celia Collopy

New York, New York State - United States

a home is a sanctuary
whether you've paced through the carpets or not
whether your confinement is voluntary, or
(like that of submarine sailors) due to external pressures
whether a man (or just a man-shaped loneliness)
shares your bed

a home is a sanctuary
despite the quiet condescension in your roommate's stare
collecting like condensation cupping your upper lip
droplets of "anti-anxiety" tea from your mother
who doesn't believe in small white pills or talk therapy
(tea is solution and savior spiced into one)

a home is a sanctuary
whether you rest, tree pose on your carpet
or cry into daisy-yellow pillow cases
whether you remember the date or your name
—or both, though neither matter anymore
as time stops and stutters on with a lurch

slouching towards Bethlehem, you move in only space
or (in this case) not much at all

a home is a sanctuary
ill-defined by plants, lemony posters, literal lemons
spilt coffee grounds, pancake batter stuck to linoleum
    countertops
swept up in a scent you no longer distinguish but one
so distinguishable from the other world with its
exhaust, gasoline and exhaustion, sweaty with fear, ill-met by
    moonlight
and populated by an agitated people

a home is a sanctuary
whether you draw open beige shades to let light in, or
swallowed in a mountain of unwashed clothes, you sleep
unabashedly unmoving under the weight of
the outdoors creeping indoors, into your sleeping dreams
seemingly lean towards horror, open air terror sinking
into your home's bones like chewed-up termite rot
an unstable foundation in the land of no where to go

because a home is a sanctuary whether you like it or not

And

Shamara Peart
Kingston, Ontario - Canada

and to start, I stick my head above the surface
and illuminate by the moonlight: my androgyny doesn't crack.
and it stays whole even when I'm trapped,
and when I'm alone
and when I'm naked.

and me, with writhing coils
and melanin armour:
and me, the last one on the river bank
and me, thawing and being thawed
and me, in the wind that rustles my dress.

and sensual sighs are exchanged between us
and now the moths in my stomach migrate
and my stuttering mouth finds yours
and our tongues waltz in languages that only we know.

and suddenly you don't want to eat dinner together
and I don't deserve the meatloaf anyway.
and I'll kill for an appetite like yours
and your face is shuttered closed

and despite tongues trembling
and sore fingers; despite soft curves
and evenings spent bent over,
we burn out.

and in a rush, me
and my smudged glasses crack.
and my body plunges itself into the biting coldness.
and I use this black-ribbon river for my plan:
and while freezing I shut my eyes
and hope that you can hear my pleas.

Bitter

Cam Ezell
Buffalo Grove, Illinois - United States

Bitter is the taste of his Jack.
Bitter is the bite of his lips.
Bitter is the loss of memory as I fall to the floor.
Bitter are the beams of filtered light.
Bitter is the chill of the bed.
Bitter is the pain of the first thrust.
Bitter is the fire of my throbbing guts.
Bitter is he in the absence of disgust.
Bitter is the clenched scream that
comes out
as one
airless

gasp.

Bitter are the tears that stain my cheeks.
Bitter is the pain of humility and anger.
Bitter are the ties that bind my innocent hands.
Bitter is the thought of death.
Bitter is his whisper, and his foul, wicked breath.

His wicked breath.

Bitter is the ghost that haunts my dreams.
Bitter is waking to see the light of day.
Bitter is the grief of a tainted sprouting Rose.
Bitter are the cries of new life.

And now in my arms rests
the bitter boy I bore.

California Rain

Therese Kosterman
Los Angeles, California - United States

Rain holds you at the window, watching.
Rain is gambled and divined.

Rain flushes worms and buried scents.
Rain is modeled, measured.

Rain scrubs light.
Rain is superstition.

Rain finds every break or basin.
Rain is war.

Rain calls wind to strip the palms.
Rain is hoarded.

Rain slides mud and flows rocks.
Rain is held and lifted over mountains.

Rain snuffs wildfire before another Paradise is lost.
Rain is squandered.

Rain leaves you, brown and lovesick.
Rain is cold.
Rain is music. rain

Die Like A Dog

Michael Angelone
Roseville, California - United States

Die like a dog –
seems like good advice,
in hindsight, under fluorescent light, with the beeps and bings.

Die like a dog –
die slowly, loved to death,
die deliberately damn it!

Die like a dog –
on the kitchen floor with short breaths, ribs through skin,
that sigh a dog takes, sighing away sadness and memory.

Die like a dog –
not taking water, not eating,
not even the good scraps.

Die like a dog – the hardest part of dying, vet says, "treatment
no cure," life with purpose now, suddenly so precious, suddenly
so sacred and pure.

Die like a dog — die
surrounded by love and memory and the soul of collective
selves.

Die like a dog — let your body wallow in my arms, unrestrained,
sloshing and basking in a cloud.

Die like a dog — without shame.

Michael Angelone

Dystonia

Sarah Dykes
Bronx, New York - United States

Dystonia, a word most people don't know
Dystonia, the cause of so much strife
Dystonia, I wish you would leave me be
Dystonia, the reason people stare at me
Dystonia, Uncontrollable you can be
Dystonia, the pain you cause me
Dystonia, my body isn't mine
Dystonia, sometimes makes my blind
Dystonia, I barely move without you
Dystonia, in spite of everything you cause
Dystonia, you don't define me

Help

Reagan Hope
Lawrence, Kansas - United States

Go. I'm
Drowning in your presence,

Go.

Go. I'm
Scratching my soul.
From off my bones.
Only to be yours.

(Go.)

I Believed You

Lisa Ochoa

Tucson, Arizona - United States

I believed you
when you said
you would
die for me.

I believed you
when you said
you would
keep us together
forever.

I believed you
when you said
you would
love me more
than anyone.

I believed you
when you said
you were sorry.

I believed you
when you said
you would
never do it again.

I believed you.

desperate, scared, longing,
begging, pleading, bleeding,
hoping, dreaming, praying,

I believed you.

I Hate Valentines

Muhammad Sobur
Ilorin - Nigeria

because they exhume from the urnful heart
the bitter remains of long-defunct memories.

because they nourish these stoical eyes
with acid—a deluge of that night seceded from home.

because they surfeit these flaccid lips
that suckled her glands with turgid, fluffy bones.

because they extort with tormenting hands
a heroic man of eros and storge,
the motherly care of a lover and
the midas touch of a father.

because they divest the soul, a cynosure of influx,
its legitimate feats with lustful longings,
oblivion with nostalgic remorse.

because they remind me of mother and of my beloved,
who relinquished their bodies,
the remembrance a morose dirge

In Times Like These

Clement Abayomi
Lagos - Nigeria

When joy flees your home
When loneliness threatens your dome
When luck locks you in futility
When dolor grips your growing glee

When sympathy licks your roof
When dejection drags you aloof
When misery seeks a seat at your door
When panic plagues you, a deluge of war

When sadness stifles your race
When tears linger long on your face
When despair drapes over your promising dreams
When fears motion in your heart like flowing streams

When a flurry of depressions preys on your heart
When the roughened paths deny you your part
You seek succor to assuage your griefs
In sickening resilience and disbeliefs

You dread troubles in struggles to cope with
A piercing pain that injures your hope,
For when you dare to make these freeze
You'll be a champion in times like these.

Inside

Mykyta Ryzhykh
Nova Kakhovka - Ukraine

You don't come home.
You don't come to the neighbors.
You don't come to me.
(You don't come to your senses.)
You don't take out the trash.
You don't clean your ears.

Looks like I died inside your head.

Intoxicating!

Chris Sako

Pahoa, Hawaii - United States

"I think I'll have another"
That's what I say,
-when it's spiked just right
-when I'll be elevated by my election
-when my selection will be soothing to my sole

"I think I'll have another"
That's what I say,
-when that six inch neck-breaker is in my possession
-when the sex appeal of that strapless leopard is roaring
-when I know, that one will make my man's heart race

"I think I'll have another"
That's what I say,
-when they sparkle and shine and call to me
-when the unassuming ask "Jimmy Chew?"
-when my weakness, my habit, my craving must be fulfilled

"I think I'll have another"
That's what I say,
-when I declare, "kittens are for children"
-when gray malt flats are needed for my trek
-when "Ugg" is all that needs to be said

"I think I'll have another"
That's what I say,
-when the pink is whispering and the red is screaming
-when I'm no longer able to resist my temptation
-when the salesclerk says, "if you take another pair, it's 25% off!"

Keeper Of Time

Sampoorna Thammadi
Jagtial, Telangana - India

Keeper of time
Could I borrow from you some time?
To make up for a past time
I won't flee the fiend this time.

Keeper of time
Show me how to travel back in time
I'll make amends and return in time
To live my future well this time.

Keeper of time
Deliver me before the appointed time
Promise, I won't make the request another time
Grant me a moment of your time.

Keeper of time
I won't live forever so, slip me through the clock
into the past between your three tiresome hands
And I know, though they say

Keeper of time
Time is cruel
Time is harsh as bad weather
Time only steals—he never gives.

Keeper of time
You are but a poor misunderstood creature
Can you make an exception for me?
I promise to tell all my friends how good you can be.

Lullaby For A Different World

Shiva R. Joyce
Labasa - Fiji

Had the bough not broken,
had the girl with the split lip not spoken,

had the oppressor been willing to relent,
had the knee not bent,

had the penny not dropped,
had opportunity not knocked,

had the bar not been fixed by colour
had the ones who held the power,
 let the unheard have their hour,

had the sign said welcome,
had the prejudice through the system,
 not framed him for a hoodlum,

had the commitment not been token,
had the change not been set in motion,
     and oceans remained (un)frozen,

Would the ripple, so small, have been felt at all,
Or simply made a different cradle of civilisation fall?

Nostalgia

Jameria Blain

Hope Mills, North Carolina - United States

To say it was a waste of time would be to puncture the heart.
To say it was the worst of times would be to misrepresent the
truth.
To say it was the best of times would be to exaggerate what
holds little merit or warmth.
To say I regret holding your hand is a lie.
To say I walked away without guilt is untrue.
To say my life has become all the better for it is accurate.
To say I've grown since our last encounter is, indeed, factual.
To say the memory of you still haunts my dreams further proves
how distance truly makes the heart fonder.

October

Donna Harlan
Jonesborough, Tennessee - United States

If trees could be proud,
in October they'd be.
If they could catwalk,
oh, the styles we'd see.

If blue could mean happy,
'twould be in the fall.
If skies could embrace you,
you'd answer their call.

If perfect beauty were achieved,
'twould be before the earth is grieved.
If autumn stayed in place of winter,
you would know 'twas God who sent her.

Penniless Asylum

Leonardo Chung
Ottawa, Illinois - United States

To be the stairs to the second floor,
slightly sunken in by passing
feet over years. To be the Christmas tree rotting
in the attic, ornamentless. To be the
sack of trash stashed inside the recycling bin,
missing the garbage truck, ripening by the hour. To be the
cracked ceramic owl roosted atop the garden,
warding no birds away as promised. To be the
crooked patio roof perched on four stone columns,
shielding ivory wicker couches from a grieving sky's tears. To be the
wooden pillar with paint scraped off careening
around in tag games, like a tetherball to be scored with. To be the
argyle sweater sitting primly in an unlabeled cardboard box,
too small to fit the family. To be the
empty Yankee Candle jars resting in the cabinets,
residue of Lemon Lavender unscraped and mellowing. To be the
black computer keyboards missing E's and A's,
R's half-rubbed off, space bar cracked, in front of dead computers.
To be the
divots in a wall of plaster. To be the
house number etched deeply into the brick,
emblazoning life with a stillness and sanctuary.

Pieces Of Me

Lisa Ochoa
Tucson, Arizona - United States

He was fond of saying

"Love you to pieces"

which never bothered her

until she started to notice

s me

      w re

           mis ing.

The pieces

that knew her own mind,

held her own place,

felt her own worth.

The pieces

that housed her dreams,

stored her hopes,

carried her pride.

The pieces

that protected her affections,

commanded respect,

maintained her ipseity.

The pieces

that stood her ground,

argued her point,

refused to back down.

The pieces

that were strong,

independent,

resilient.

She could not recall

where she'd last seen them

when she'd lost them,

how they'd been taken

or if, in her shame, she simply

gave
        them
                away.

Rain In My Cucumber Garden

Abigail Maurer
Fort Wayne, Indiana - United States

Sunshine shone around the yard.
Sunshine warmed me on that chilly day.
Sunshine lit the garden where I worked.
Sunshine glittered on my bowl as I picked the cucumbers.
Sunshine eliminated the ground and vines.
Sunshine made it easy to see the vegetables.

Rain, suddenly, without warning began to fall.
Rain drenched me in cold water as it poured from the sky.
Rain fell so quickly it bounced on the cucumbers.
Rain flowing in little streams down the vines through the garden.
Rain, because of it I dart for shelter.
Rain lasting for only minutes.

Wind chases away the clouds.
Wind blows them away as quickly as they came.
Wind makes the leaves rustle.
Wind causes the water to fall from the trees.
Wind shakes the canopy where I seek shelter.
Wind brings back the sunshine.

Sunshine returns as quickly as it left.
Sunshine brings a beautiful rainbow.
Sunshine dries the garden as I return to the cucumbers.
Sunshine allows me to resume my work.
Sunshine as if the rain had never come.
Sunshine shines around the yard.

Slow Burns

Shams Alkamil
Austin, Texas - United States

I was raised with creaky rooftop doors
& Arabian dust that kisses
decade old swings.
On the side of town where dark-skinned
migrants walk with hunched backs,
stacked from native bricks, making homes on
our vertebrae.
Al-Naseem: wake of the grieving.

Here, with all this love,
there is nobody but me and my golden family of 8
counting riyals & feeding
grandma the love she sacrificed.
Sharing immigrant blankets,
painted with the newest edition
of lions and crows.
Here, with all this love.

I was raised with too-thin
coats and too-heavy accents,
& while we undress our assimilation
at dinnertime; How do we undress our
bricked vertebrae?

Here, with all this love,
there is nobody but me
and sisterhood. One sings
jaded eighth notes, another whole notes.
Careful to hold nectar
spaces & make room for mistakes.
Here, with all this love.

I was raised with slogans
of promising I'll be naked for a man,
& playing naive when he found
parasites left from another.
Too many slogans & I want a divorce;
sign the papers with the blood
t(he)y drained from my body.

Here, with all this love,
there is nobody but me and me.
Hurl the bricked vertebrae &
giggle as the mirror shatters.
Stick surgical-glue, patch
by patch on C1-L5.
& await the slow burn.

That Did Not Happen

Stephanie Harris Mercado
Fresno, California - United States

I did it
Sent that letter today
Cried all night long
Wished that the mail returned unopened

    But it did not

I did it
Told her what happened
The letter–all shameful details
Hoped it shocked her

    She shrugged it off

I did it
Warned her about him
An adulterer, abusive
Prayed it would cause a rift

    She married him last weekend

I did it
Gave her our pictures
He showed me—love hurts
Believed that would do the job

   They are going to have a child

I did it
Spoke to him again
Faced him one last time
Knowing that would make me stronger

   I need his love

I did it
Said I love him
And she said it too
Should've made us both leave

   But that didn't happen

The Chant Of The Irish Immigrant

Mary Bean
Columbia, South Carolina - United States

I AM BOADECIA.
I am naked, stained blue
and slashed red
by Rome's ballistas.

I AM BOADECIA.
I am man with machine gun
hidden in horseshit
from British soldiers.

I AM BOADECIA.
I am skeletal child
crawling up cliffs to
watch potatoes sail to Scotland.

I AM BOADECIA.
I am Celtic cross on
bloodstained altar
crumbling to dust.

I AM BOADECIA.
I am criminal caged by
washboards and hung on
clotheslines scrubbed with soap.

I AM BOADECIA.
I am spillage of corpses
shoveled by nuns
into mass graves.

I AM BOADECIA.
I am crystal drops of salt
mined in New York
sweatshops.

I AM BOADECIA.
I am carpenter in clouds
crafting temples of steel
to slash the sky wide open.

I AM BOADECIA.
I am Aengus soft afloat
with feathers white
from stars dripping milk.

And you, my lovely,
kiss my feet and
braid my hair into
a copper crown.

FOR I AM BOADECIA.
AND I AM STILL ALIVE.

The Greats

Grace Greer
North Augusta, South Carolina - United States

I will fly a plane colored ruby red, and cover earth with roses.

I will paint a submarine and its adventures through the darkened sea, while chewing, popping gum.

I will write my longest story about cliches and tropes and treasures all in erasable marker.

I will crush bones to dust for a set in my movie, starring everyone famous except for me.

I will buy a pet platypus just to prove I am not a cat nor dog.

I will not fool you into thinking I'm original, when I already have.

I will and I will not take credit for this poem.

The Thorn's Wish

Katherine Musgrave
New York, New York State - United States

The sentience of neutrality snarls, sinking its teeth into those who approach it
The sentience of neutrality sneers at those subsisting in survival
The sentience of survival lulls in its peace

The sentience of neutrality continues to remind us: thorns don't care who they prick.

The sentience of sound melts, and what's left stands as frozen ice,
The sentience of silence remains alone, screaming: "Remember, my love, play nice."

The sentience within us all evades us more than we reveal,
The sentience we defend and we cling to, the sentience we steal.

The sentience of neutrality pervades every identity,
    The sentience holds a wish.
The sentience of neutrality yearns to take a stance,
    The sentience is forced remiss.

Trust

Amanda Fozzy

High Ridge, Missouri - United States

I'm not saying I have trust issues
I'm just saying I'm a little jumpy.
I'm just saying don't touch me.
I'm just saying stay out of my space.
I'm just saying I carry lightning in my pocket like my life depends
on it
I'm just saying my favorite lipstick will send you to the hospital.
I'm just saying my chains have made me stronger in every way
And I'm more capable than I look.
I'm not saying I have trust issues.
I'm just saying if you try to hurt me I'm ready
And I will not be the victim again.

Under Water

Mi-Ka Nam
Rio Rancho, New Mexico - United States

Take me down beneath the water
Take me down, take me deep
Take me down beneath the water
Take me down, where I can feel
Take me down beneath the water
Take me down, a time to heal
Take me down beneath the water
Take me down, so I can sleep
Take me down beneath the water
Take me down, take me deep.

Dear Reader,

We are ecstatic to note that you chose to read one of our publications. The time you invested into reading this book is much appreciated. We value your allegiance. As a give back present, we will be happy to share **'YOUR PICTURE HOLDING THIS BOOK'** on our *Official Social Media Handles* such as Facebook, Instagram and Twitter.

All you have to do is – send it to us.

1. Write Your Name

2. Review, if any

3. Subject Line of Email – Pic Holding Book (Book Name)

4. Image Attached – jpeg / gif/ png file.

Email it to – <u>poetschoice@hotmail.com</u>

Send Us A Book Review

Now, you can send us your written or video – *book review.*

If it is a written review, we will use your review in the book when it goes for a reprint, with your name included. So, please do remember to specify your name.

If it is a video, we will showcase your video on our Youtube Channel. Do subscribe to our Youtube Channel 'Poets Choice' for more. You can reach us your video review via email.

Email – poetschoice@hotmail.com

Subject – Video/Written Book Review _____Seasoned Women

Please try to include, in your email –

1.   The date you purchased the book.
2.   What was your take away.
3.   Why did you like/dislike our book.
4.   What makes you come back to us.
5.   Is there anything you find *different*, something that is specific or unique in our books, something that stands out.

Our Anthologies

Our Single Author Publications:

| A Futile Attempt At Delaying The Inevitable | Burnout | Blunder Down Under | Free Air Berlin | Homelessness |

| The Joy of Seasons | Mother Medusa | Seasoned Women | Summers In Laurel Canyon | Sunlight Reflector |

| Questions We Didn't Ask Out Loud | Unheard Whispers | Walking Through The Four Seasons | Where Have All The Bluejays Gone | Whispers In The Wind |

CPSIA information can be obtained
at www.ICGtesting.com
Printed in the USA
LVHW031221220323
742255LV00010B/566